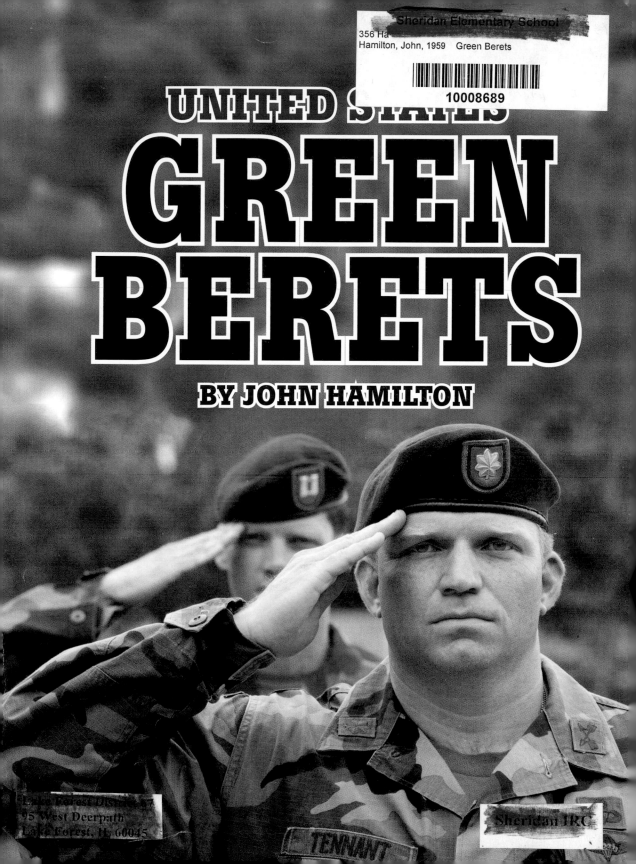

UNITED STATES
GREEN BERETS

BY JOHN HAMILTON

TENNANT

VISIT US AT
WWW.ABDOPUBLISHING.COM

Published by ABDO Publishing Company, 8000 West 78th Street, Suite 310, Edina, MN 55439. Copyright ©2012 by Abdo Consulting Group, Inc. International copyrights reserved in all countries. No part of this book may be reproduced in any form without written permission from the publisher. A&D Xtreme™ is a trademark and logo of ABDO Publishing Company.

Printed in the United States of America, North Mankato, Minnesota.
062011
092011

Editor: Sue Hamilton
Graphic Design: Sue Hamilton
Cover Design: John Hamilton
Cover Photo: Getty Images
Interior Photos: AP-pgs 9-11; Defense Video & Imagery Distribution System-pgs 2-5, 20-23, & 26-31; Department of Defense-pgs 6-7, 14-15, 18-19; Getty Images-pg 1; U.S. Army-pgs 12-13, 16-17, 24-25 & 32; Wikimedia-pg 8.

Library of Congress Cataloging-in-Publication Data

Hamilton, John, 1959-
 Green Berets / John Hamilton.
     p. cm. -- (United States armed forces)
 Includes index.
 ISBN 978-1-61783-066-2
 1. United States. Army. Special Forces--Juvenile literature. I. Title.
 UA34.S64H353 2012
 356'.167--dc23
                         2011018114

CONTENTS

GREEN BERETS

The Special Forces are a part of the United States Army. They are a special operations force. Their nickname is the Green Berets because of the distinctive headgear they often wear. Green Beret troops are some of the best-trained fighters in the U.S. military.

XTREME FACT

The main mission of the Green Berets is to train foreign military forces to defend their country and the interests of the United States. The Green Berets are both warriors and ambassadors.

The Green Berets are specialists in unconventional warfare. They can operate in small groups deep in enemy territory for long stretches of time. When dangerous, top-secret missions are required, the Green Berets are among the first to be sent in.

Special Forces soldiers fast-rope into a combat zone from the back of a V-22 Osprey tiltrotor aircraft.

XTREME FACT

The Green Berets' motto is the Latin phrase *De Oppresso Liber*, which means "To Liberate the Oppressed."

HISTORY

The Green Berets trace their roots to the U.S. Army's Office of Strategic Services (OSS). The OSS was formed during World War II. OSS troops worked deep in German- and Japanese-controlled territory, gathering information, ambushing the enemy, and training local resistance fighters.

Above: General William Donovan, head of the Office of Strategic Services, reviews a group of OSS soldiers in 1945.
Left: Colonel Aaron Bank was a co-founder of the modern Army Special Forces.

In 1952, the United States Army Special Forces were formed. Their unique dark-green headgear was based on berets worn by elite British commandos. The mission of the Special Forces was to conduct guerrilla warfare and train foreign armies to fight the enemies of the United States.

A Special Forces unit trains for military duties around the world in 1962.

U.S. Special Forces soldiers move past the wreckage of enemy tanks and equipment in Vietnam in 1969.

The Green Berets were very active in Southeast Asia during the Vietnam War. Later, they disrupted drug traffickers in Colombia and other Central American countries. They fought during the invasion of Panama in 1989. They have also fought in the War on Terror in countries that include Iraq and Afghanistan.

XTREME FACT
President John F. Kennedy said the green beret that Army Special Forces soldiers wear is "a symbol of excellence, a badge of courage, a mark of distinction in the fight for freedom."

TRAINING

The U.S. Army Special Forces are among the best-trained troops in the world. Green Beret recruits undergo extreme physical conditioning. Intelligence and resourcefulness are also required. Candidates learn advanced combat skills. Recruits also master foreign languages in order to train forces in other countries.

Special Forces members train for high-altitude jumps by leaping out of airplanes at 6,000 feet (1,829 m).

Right: Training in military mountaineering teaches Green Berets how to reach high-terrain objectives.

WEAPONS & EQUIPMENT

The Green Berets fight with standard Army infantry weapons, such as the M16 assault rifle. They may also use specialized equipment, such as the M4 carbine with attached grenade launcher.

A shell casing is ejected from an M4 rifle.

XTREME FACT
Depending on the mission, other Green Beret equipment might include GPS locators, satellite communications gear, scuba gear, night vision goggles, and HALO helmets, which are used for high-altitude parachute jumps.

A Special Forces soldier descends in a parachute during a combined American/Canadian military exercise near Mt. Rainier in Washington state.

SURVIVAL SKILLS

The Green Berets are trained to fight and survive in almost any environment. They may travel to their targets by air, land, or sea. Green Berets can be dropped by parachute deep in enemy territory. They can survive off the land for weeks at a time, whether they are in forests, steamy jungles, deserts, mountains, or even frozen Arctic lands.

A-TEAMS

The Green Berets are organized into small groups called A-Teams, or Operational Detachments-A (ODA). Each A-Team consists of 12 men, including 2 officers and 10 sergeants. Team members are cross-trained in various skills, such as weapons, medical, and communications.

XTREME FACT

A-Team members can speak in foreign languages, and can operate in the field for long periods of time without help or supervision.

RECONNAISSANCE

A Special Forces group is extracted from a mountaintop in Afghanistan after performing a mission to disrupt enemy communications.

Before an attack by U.S. military forces, the Green Berets often sneak undetected behind enemy lines. They uncover as much information as possible about the enemy, including troop strength, weapons, and movement. They send this crucial data back to their commanders so that U.S. forces can prepare more effective strikes.

XTREME FACT

Army Special Forces were sent to Afghanistan weeks before the U.S. invasion in October 2001. Their covert information gathering greatly helped in the effort to topple the Taliban and al-Qaeda terrorist networks.

TRAINING FOREIGN TROOPS

Training foreign troops to fight enemy forces is called "foreign internal defense." It is one of the Green Berets' most important jobs. They assist, train, and organize foreign soldiers to defend their homeland as well as fight the enemies of the United States.

An Afghan policeman is taught how to use a grenade launcher.

XTREME FACT

During the Cold War, the Green Berets helped foreign armies fight Communist aggressors. Today, the Green Berets assist many countries, such as Colombia and Afghanistan, to fight drug traffickers and terrorists.

DE OPPRESSO LIBER

DIRECT ACTION

The Green Berets use the element of surprise to perform lightning-fast "direct action" missions. These might include attacking enemy troops, destroying equipment, blowing up bridges, disrupting communications, or rescuing soldiers held in foreign lands.

Firebombs are set off in an Iraqi palm grove to destroy hidden enemy weapons and explosives.

COUNTER-TERRORISM

Special Forces soldiers clear a room during a counterterrorism exercise in Baghdad, Iraq.

One of the missions of the United States Army Special Forces is to fight terrorist activities in foreign lands. The Green Berets are specially trained in hostage rescue and advanced combat techniques such as fast-roping into dangerous enemy areas.

XTREME FACT
Green Berets try to stop terrorists before they can strike. They work with U.S. allies in foreign countries to hunt down terrorists, disrupt their networks, cut off their money supplies, and bring them to justice.

Special Forces members and Afghan commandos begin a mission to capture homemade explosives in Kandahar Province, Afghanistan.

THE FUTURE

Special operations soldiers call themselves "The Quiet Professionals." The Green Berets usually work in secret. Most of their success stories will remain untold. But modern warfare depends more often on covert, small-unit operations instead of large-scale battles. The Green Berets are well-trained for the toughest missions. Whatever future challenges await, the Green Berets will meet them head-on.

GLOSSARY

Assault Rifle

Assault rifles are the most commonly used weapons used by today's armed forces. They use medium-power cartridges (the part containing the bullet), and are fired from the shoulder. Soldiers can either fire the weapon in semiautomatic mode (one shot or short burst every time the trigger is pulled), or in fully automatic (the weapon fires rapidly until the trigger is released or ammo runs out). The U.S. Army's main assault rifles are the M16 and M4 carbine.

Commando

Commandos are highly trained soldiers who specialize in raids, sometimes using techniques such as rappelling or parachuting to reach their targets. Commandos often use stealth to attack the enemy. They are also sometimes used to rescue hostages.

Cold War

A period of tension and hostility between the United States and its allies versus the Soviet Union, China, and their allies after World War II. The Cold War ended after the Soviet Union collapsed in 1991.

Covert

A military action that is concealed, and not publicly acknowledged.

Fast-Rope

A troop-insertion technique in which soldiers descend a thick rope that hangs from a helicopter. Fast-roping is required for places where helicopters cannot land, or there is too much enemy activity for them to land. Troops wearing gloves slide down the rope using their hands to control their descent. The technique can be very dangerous, especially if a soldier is carrying heavy equipment.

Guerrilla Warfare

Small groups of fighters (sometimes civilians instead of soldiers) who use the element of surprise and mobility to achieve their objectives. Teams of guerillas excel at ambushes and sabotage.

Scuba

Equipment that allows divers to breath underwater without a hose attached to the surface or other air supply. Scuba stands for "self contained underwater breathing apparatus."

Special Operations

Military forces that use unconventional warfare. They are usually organized in small groups and use stealth, speed, and surprise to achieve their objectives. Special operations soldiers are highly trained and self reliant while on the battlefield.

Vietnam War

A conflict between the countries of North Vietnam and South Vietnam from 1955-1975. Communist North Vietnam was supported by China and the Soviet Union. The United States entered the war on the side of South Vietnam.

INDEX